A Place on Water

Also by the authors:

A Place on Water

ESSAYS

Robert Kimber, Wesley McNair
Bill Roorbach

TILBURY HOUSE, PUBLISHERS
Gardiner, Maine

Tilbury House, Publishers
2 Mechanic Street • Gardiner, Maine 04345
800-582-1899 • www.tilburyhouse.com

First printing: March 2004
10 9 8 7 6 5 4 3 2 1

                  Cataloging-in-Publication Data
Kimber, Robert.
   A place on water / essays by Robert Kimber, Wesley McNair,
and Bill Roorbach.
      p. cm
   ISBN 0-88448-262-6 (pbk. : alk. paper)
   1. Ponds--Maine. 2. Natural history--Maine. I. McNair,
Wesley. II. Roorbach, Bill. III. Title.
QH98.K5 2004
508.741--dc22   2003026577

Cover designed on Crummett Mountain by Edith Allard,
Somerville, Maine.
Printing and binding by Maple Vail, Kirkwood, New York.

For Rita, Diane, and Juliet

PONDSIDE

The canoe shadow
by the still canoe bends
and wiggles

and straightens. Fifty feet
out from the camp
on the far shore,

a brown boat
with a green cabin
floats among inverted

birches. Where
does it come from,
this growing island

of waves, this wind
within windlessness?
In the feathery, exact

reflection of a spruce
surrounded by
a twilight sky,

one circle,
then a second opens
to the under world.

—Wesley McNair

Contents

Drury Pond: An Idyll

Robert Kimber

At the pond I imbibe both the sweetness of solitude and the sweetness of society. I also imbibe, on the porch of Wes and Diane's camp, an occasional beer, which adds a nip of hops to the largely mellow flavor of our conversations.

That Wes and Diane would be here, would in

fact own this camp on the pond and by that owning add infinitely to the pleasure Rita and I take in this place that has long been one of our favorite places on earth, was not too long ago not at all certain.

They were in search of a place on water. I knew that, for I had visited with Wes several other places they were considering, none of which proved suitable. All those rejected places had neighbors too close or were intrinsically too tacky (interior walls of that plastic stuff that fakes wood paneling, accordion closet doors also of plastic), places located on little dirt roads at the head of which the visitor found six or a dozen or more signs nailed to a tree: Jones, Halleck, Dimbaugh, Crumpworth, Doodlebecker, Heep, Humbert, Smith, etc., each sign indicating that on this road Jones, Halleck, etc. each owned a camp, Halleck's camp cheek by jowl with Dimbaugh's and so on down the line.

Do we want this camp for peace and quiet, Wes and Diane had to ask themselves, or do we want to watch water skiers roar by behind their forty-horse Yamaha outboards? Do we want invitations to the Crumpworths' Fourth-of-July barbecue parties complete with firecrackers, sparklers, and hamburgers underdone on the propane grill? Do we want hearty laughter, conviviality, Reverend Whipsnack's account of climbing Pike's Peak with his lean, mean, twenty-six-year-old son and platinum blonde, long-legged daughter-in-law: "They thought they'd leave the old man huffing and puffing behind in the dust, but they had another think coming. Oh, I gave them a run for their money and then some. Ha, ha. Ho, ho."

How important, after all, is a flush toilet, electricity, a telephone? Isn't the point *not* to watch the TV, *not* to stay in touch with students, secretaries, deans, plumbers, electricians?

Of course that's the point, Wes agreed, but

peace and quiet and plumbing and electricity don't have to be mutually exclusive, do they? So when Dick Vaughan told me he wanted to sell his camp on the pond—the most perfect camp, by the way, on this most perfect of ponds, a camp at the north end of the pond and so perfectly situated that, sitting on the porch, you can look south down the length of this small, barely half-mile pond onto the mountain rising beyond and can watch the sun come up over the eastern shore and watch it drop in the west, casting shadows of the tall white pines out onto the water as early as four on a summer afternoon while here, at this camp, you can still bask in sunshine on the dock—when Dick told me he wanted to sell this camp, I told him I knew somebody who might be interested; but I was not hopeful. No flush, no electricity.

Wes and I went to have a look at the place one afternoon. Wes stands six foot three; this camp appears to have been built by the Seven Dwarfs. In the master bedroom upstairs there's barely room to walk around the double bed and fit in a dresser; the bedroom next to it is snugger still; and a third cubbyhole houses a double-decker bunk. Going downstairs, even I, at five eight, have to duck so I don't bang my head. Downstairs, living/dining room and kitchenette all share a space about twenty by twelve feet.

As self-appointed real-estate broker, I put a positive spin on the camp's dimensions.

"Cozy, isn't it?" I observed, but I was thinking "cramped."

Wes nodded. He moved around cautiously, concerned, I imagined, not only about conking his head in the stairwell or on the wrought-iron chandelier over the table but also about banging his funny bone, shouldering candlesticks off the mantlepiece, barking his shins, stubbing his toes. Wes wears size fourteen shoes. Even his feet are too big for this place. Wes has written a poem about those outsized feet that have had to put up with a lot of ribbing in their time, as have the shoes that shod them—clodhoppers, platters, skis.

                            Unconcerned with fitting in,
all you have ever wanted was to take me in the direction
of my own choosing. Never mind the hands
getting all the attention as they wave to others
on the street, this is not their poem,
but only yours, steady vessels, who all along
have resisted my desire to be like everyone else,
who turn after the hands are done and carry me
with resolute steps into my separate life.

Where else, I wondered, but away from this small building would those resolute steps carry him? No plumbing, no electricity, and barely enough room for a big man to stand up or turn around.

What a pity, I thought; what a goddam crying shame. What wouldn't I give to have Wes and Diane our neighbors here, right next door to our own patch of land on this our favorite pond where, on just about every summer day, we come for a late-afternoon swim? Diane, who did not hesitate, when some creep in a Roman bus groped her daughter, to hit the guy over the head with her pocketbook; who brought us, one Easter, a little basket complete with frizzy cellophane grass, jelly beans, little yellow marshmallow chicks, and a couple of bunnies made of solid dark chocolate; Diane, whose red hair erupts from her head like molten lava, overflow from her warm and fiery heart.

And instead of—or as well as—meeting Wes for beers in the brew pub in Farmington, we could meet on this very camp porch. Here, as the breeze died of a summer evening and the pond turned into a placid mirror and the hermit thrushes poured out their harmonies in the woods around us, we could raise our voices in celebration of the kingfisher's chattering flight, the word well chosen, the comma well placed, the yearling moose feeding in the lily pads, the murmur of Rita and Diane's talk down on the dock. We could also plot the downfall of all who deserve to fall down: Republicans, for example, and stuffed shirts and people who call too many meetings and write too many memos. Never mind that our plots will come to naught, that all the sonsabitches who ought to be in eclipse are instead at the zenith of their wretched powers. Never mind any of that.

Ah, Wes, you great ambling bear with feet to match the size of your soul, you old silvertip with your grizzled beard, your faded jeans, your Red Sox baseball cap, what a joy to think we might grow old together right here, walking these woods, sharing our loves and rages.

But after that first walk-through at the camp I was not hopeful.

"Well," Rita asked me when I came home, "what do you think?"

"Not a prayer," I said. "No plumbing, no electricity, and the place is too dinky. Have you ever watched a giraffe trying to get comfortable in a submarine?"

When I call this pond the most perfect of ponds, I should add that its perfection lies largely, if not wholly, in the eyes of a very few beholders. Nothing here speaks of the high-value, upscale vacation experience. Fisherfolk will find no trout or salmon here, only sunfish and yellow perch and an occasional small pickerel, fish you can catch in any old warm-water pond anywhere. Tiny, tucked into the hills, hunched down, the pond is too small for even the smallest sailboat or motorboat.

Speed and power are useless here. There are no grand vistas, no broad panoramas, nothing at all for the wide screen. Like a porcupine, the pond is small, modest, unassuming, unglamourous, an unpretentious beast with prickly perimeter defenses that discourage most folks from seeking close association. Its entire west shore is so steep that even walking there, much less erecting any kind of structure, defies both gravity and common sense. At either end of that shore, a few semi-flat places not much bigger than a golf green harbor a few camps: John and Joanne Judson's, Jarmila Vogel's, ours. The inlet bog forms an impassable moat at much of the north end. The outlet bog covers half the east shore and hooks around the south end. The remainder of the east shore is as steep as the west, except for a few hundred yards midway down the pond where the hillside flattens out enough to admit four camps.

Modest and unpretentious as the pond itself, these camps were built with a tact their present owners maintain. "We are here," these buildings say, "not to reshape this place in our own image but to let it shape us, not to teach this place a lesson but to let it teach us. We are here not to make noise but to be quiet, to listen and watch." Everyone who owns a camp on the pond adheres to that code. The only boats here are canoes and rowboats. There are no electronic horrors, no boom boxes. If you swim or paddle near Bill Meyer's place on a hot August afternoon, you might hear the Red Sox game drifting softly out to you through his open windows. The only other sounds generated by human beings are the comforting, companionable ones of kids splashing happily on the tiny beach at the Greens' camp, the thunk of an oar on a gunwale.

But to say the pond lacks glamour is not to deny it beauty. Its beauty is so clear and bright because it is not painted over—no lipstick, no mascara. Like a carrot pulled from the garden and eaten on the spot, it brings the tastes of sun, earth, and rain right to you unadorned. The pond is a miniature couched in its oval frame of hills. You can hold it in your two hands; the whole picture and every detail in it are visible at once. A patch of mist forms over the water, then dissipates. A swamp maple on the shore blazes up fiery red in mid-October.

At first glance, in other words, the pond may seem pleasant enough but no great shakes. At second glance, it starts to grow on you. At third and fourth glance, it really gets under your skin. At fifth and sixth and beyond, you realize you're undergoing a slow, osmotic process: The pond is getting into your blood. The prospect of living without the pond in your life is too awful to contemplate. Finally, you realize, you're in love.

When Wes came back for a second look, then for a third and a fourth, I figured the place had to have gotten under his skin, too. We continued to have some pro-forma talk about electricity. Dick and Peg Vaughan, both being advanced in age and neither of them in the best of health, had not wanted to be without a telephone, so they had engineered a phone line that ran underwater across the cove from Bill Meyer's place to theirs.

"Couldn't we do that with a power line?" Wes asked.

"I don't see why not," I said, always the upbeat broker. "If Cyrus W. Field could get a telegraph cable laid across the floor of the Atlantic Ocean from Ireland to Newfoundland, we can lay a few hundred yards of wire underwater from Bill Meyer's to you."

Wes had softened noticeably. I could already see the look of fond ownership on his face. This talk of submarine wire was academic. His eyes and mind were on other things. He was seeing the white pines towering up on either side of the porch, way too big in circumference for even a long-armed man like him to reach around. Inside, he was admiring the fieldstone fireplaces, one downstairs and one up in the master bedroom, each stone, like each word in a good poem, sharp and distinct in its own shape and grain yet tied in and linked to every other. He was listening to the clear, non-electrified silence surrounding the ovenbird's call. He was hooked.

"Gosh," Dick Vaughan said to me a couple of days later, "I hope your friends take the place. We can't imagine anybody we'd rather see have it."

"Nor can we, Dick," I said. "Nor can we."

Summer is the time of society at the pond; winter, the time of solitude. The society we started with was our own—Rita; our son, Greg; our dog, Lucy; me—though without the society of the Judsons, we never would have come to know the pond ourselves. About twenty years ago, our post-master told me the Judsons owned that tiny pond-side camp you could just barely see from the road. I found that an intriguing tidbit of Isn't-It-a-Small-World intelligence because some twenty years before, in 1965, I had met John and Joanne Judson at a dinner party in Waterville. But in the several years we had lived in Temple, we had never seen a sign of life at the Judsons' camp. They lived, the postmaster said, in Wisconsin and came to Temple only rarely. When I finally did see a car parked there one August afternoon, I didn't pass up the chance to reconnect.

"Sure I remember," John said, "the Fullams' house, August 1965. You were just about to leave for Germany."

We reminisced, compared notes. John was teaching English at the University of Wisconsin/ La Crosse, right smack on the Mississippi River. For many years he and Joanne had been editing and publishing a little magazine called *Northeast*. John had been an all-around athlete in his youth: football, baseball, track. He still looked it, his graying black hair trimmed short to fit under a helmet, the compact, solid body of a quarterback who bounces off tacklers like a hard rubber ball.

"You guys should come swim," he said, "whether we're here or not. It'd be nice to know someone's enjoying the place."

And we did, we did. Late every summer afternoon we went there. We swam across to the great raft of lily pads that skirts the bog on the east shore; then we turned left and swam along the shore. Lucy—part black Lab, part spaniel, part seal maybe—was way ahead of us. Every day she charged out of the water at the little point where Bob Morris's camp sits tucked into a grove of big pines. She raced around in search of red squirrels, chickadees, chipmunks, anything to bark at. When we touched bottom at the point and headed back to Judsons', Lucy gave up her hunt, leapt into the water in a gleeful geyser, and chuffed out ahead of us again.

Somewhere out in the middle, immersed in the cooling but not too cold water warmed by the August sun, either Rita or I would repeat one of our pond mantras, something like: "It doesn't get any better than this, does it?" But, translated, all our mantras meant: "Ah, my beloved mate, have we not found the Earthly Paradise? So what if the house needs paint again and the clutch just went on the Subaru? Greg is a young man of kind and generous heart; Lucy, the world's prettiest, most sweet-natured black mutt. And here we are, all four of us, afloat in the world's most perfect pond."

As we neared the western shore, Rita cruised the blueberry bushes growing there. All through the season, she plucked the day's ripened berries and, still afloat, ate them. She was a shore bird feeding, an aquatic deer grazing.

Poor Judsons! Only two, maybe three weeks a year they had free to spend here, and we dove off their dock every day from early June until early September, sometimes even into early October in a really warm fall. How could we possibly right that awful inequity?

The dock was pretty rickety, so I cut three big cedars on our place and hauled them down to the pond, where my new pal, Bill Roorbach, helped me assemble them into a new floating dock. Every fall, I pulled the dock out of the water with a come-along. Every spring, I launched it again and anchored it to the shore. Around Christmastime I called John and Joanne out there on the banks of the Mississippi and reported that all was well at their camp on the pond.

But of course there is nothing we can do for them that will ever balance their gift to us of those many afternoon swims.

Six years ago, our neighbor Sandy Gregor told us she'd seen an ad in the *Franklin Journal* for a camp and acre of land for sale on the pond. The price was way too high. We didn't even want a camp. All we wanted was a little piece of land on the water so that we could always, always, no matter what, have access to this tiny, unprepossessing, most perfect of ponds.

I cursed and bellowed about the camp. "Rita!" I said. "I can't stand owning another building. I never want to saw another board! I never want to pound another nail! Look at the roof!"

The roof—covered with ancient, dried-out, shrunken roofing paper—leaked. I could see daylight through it. I could see rotting boards in it.

"Will we ever again in this life," she said, "have a chance to buy a piece of land on the pond? Camp or no camp? Leaky roof or no leaky roof?"

"Most likely not," I had to admit.

"So?" she said.

So we bought it. And the next fall, I swung around on climbing ropes, peeled the old roofing paper off, pulled four million roofing nails, built scaffolding, dropped a scaffolding plank on my own dumb head, yanked out rotting roof boards, nailed in new ones, laid tar paper, climbed up and down ladders, laid row upon row upon row of green three-tab asphalt shingles over the tar paper.

Lucy came with me every day, my sole help and support. She couldn't do much in a practical way, but her presence gave endless comfort. She rambled the hillside and settled down on the pine needles for snoozes.

When life up on the roof became too grim and wearisome, I would holler down to her: "Hey, Miss Dog! Hey, Ms. Lucy Poo!"

She would wag her tail and, along with it, her whole black, floppy-eared self. She would bark. "Come on down, man, and do something sensible. Let's take a walk. Let's go for a swim."

Now, some five years later, with the trials of the roof job faded into the past and dear Lucy, alas, in her grave, I have to say that roof gives me great pleasure. Every time we walk to the camp on the narrow, shaded trail that leads to it, I admire my own handiwork, those neat rows of green shingles I laid while Lucy cheered me up and cheered me on. By now, I'm totally reconciled to this building I didn't want. I'm downright fond of it. The screened-in porch reaches nearly to the water's edge, but pine, hemlock, and birch in front of the building and surrounding it make it nearly invisible from the pond. The place has the feel of a bird's nest, well camouflaged but affording a high, leafy vantage point for viewing the world.

The moral of this story? If you get a chance to spend too much money on a goofy, extravagant, self-indulgent enterprise, don't let a leaky roof stand in your way.

Owning our own place on the pond now, we extend open invitations to friends to come swim whenever they like, as John and Joanne did for us. Bill Roorbach and Juliet Karlsen and their dogs, Wally and Desi, come often but usually later than our four-thirty or five o'clock swim, so we usually miss them. And if we do meet, most likely Rita and I will just be climbing up the dock ladder or on shore toweling off when Wally and Desi, the advance guard, come racing down the hill.

Desi, neat, trim, short-haired, black and white, has the air of a nervous middle-aged butler charged with keeping a hyperactive teenager out of trouble. Wally is no longer a teenager, but he still acts like one. A shaggy, long-eared spaniel and who-knows-what-else mix, he's all panting, pink-tongued exuberance. If you're not braced for him, he can bowl you over with his sixty-plus pounds of cannonball love. In the water, propelled by his broad retriever paws, he chugs along tirelessly, the image of unsinkable buoyancy. He's a furry aircraft carrier. You could land jet fighters on his back.

Water is not Desi's element. He approaches it cautiously, and only when it's clear that Bill and Juliet and Wally are heading out for a long, leisurely swim and that he'll be left behind does he overcome his reluctance and tiptoe in. For every one stroke of Wally's wide paws, skinny-legged Desi has to take three or four. Wally wallows and revels in the water. Desi churns frantically in it. He's trying to climb out and run on top. Go for a swim? He'd prefer a walk, thank you.

But sometimes we do all arrive together, and while Wally plops off the end of the dock and Desi frets at the watery prospect before him, we humans shed sneakers and shirts on the downed log that serves as our dockside bench. Bill wears raggedy cut-off jeans for swim trunks and his hair pulled back in a ponytail. He has a high, domed forehead, a downright Shakespearian forehead, lots of room in that brain for concocting ingenious plots, fashioning fine-tuned sentences. Bill is the guy every hippie ought to become when he grows up, just as open to the world and adventuresome as any youngster but with none of the flakiness that dogs most middle-aged hippies. He combines the élan of the amateur with the highly developed skills of the master. Whether he's remodeling his kitchen or writing a short story, his work is elegant in its conception, solid in its construction, flawless in its finish work.

But here at the pond, we're not working. Our medium is neither wood nor words but water. As all six of us—four humans, two dogs—swim out from the shade of the hill into the sunlight, we're like a school of dolphins or a family of otters. We're nowhere near as skillful swimmers as those aquatic acrobats; but water seems to affect us as it does them, making us more sociable and playful. Blood is thicker than water, but water is thicker than air. In the kind of non-competitive swimming we do in the pond, water conducts the currents of our friendship back and forth between us. We converse silently through the ripples and wakes our fins and flippers and paws trail behind us, and if we do speak, our words sound a bit like the murmuring gabble of a raft of ducks or, if we're clowning and boisterous, like the hooting of loons.

Swimmingly—that's how summertime goes at the pond. The summer of 2000 proved one of fresh starts that all went swimmingly, the summer when Wes and Diane deliberated about the Vaughans' camp, bought it, and settled into it with all the chattering glee of house wrens building a nest, also the summer when Juliet was pregnant with Elysia, who would be born in September.

Slim, blonde, and lithe, Juliet the swimmer has always reminded me of Venus in Botticelli's most famous painting, which I now retitled in my own mind as "The Birth of Venus about to Give Birth." If outside influences—the music an expectant mother hears, the tranquillity or agitation of her days—do in fact help determine an infant's temperament, then it seemed to me Elysia was destined to be the most cheerful of children. Not only were her prenatal days filled with the voices of adults eager to welcome her into the world; but, on nearly every summer afternoon, she would also be doubly upheld, afloat in the womb and in the pond. Juliet remarked more than once what a pleasure swimming was to her in those late months of her pregnancy, how light she felt in the water.

Okay: The sunny, even-keeled disposition

Elysia has displayed in her first years of life owes much more to her parentage than it does to her mom's prenatal swims, but I like to think that being cradled often in these friendly waters contributed in some small way to Elysia's buoyant nature.

The first inklings of solitude come in September. Early frosts cool the water. The four camps across the pond are buttoned up for the coming winter. Wes and I begin our polar-bear contest: Which one of us will be dumb and stubborn enough to keep swimming until ice starts forming between our toes?

It's about three o'clock on an October afternoon and unseasonably warm even for this stretch of mild Indian summer days. Our place on the west shore is already deep in shadow that extends well out into the pond. Where there is no sun, the water is noticeably cooler, so I swim off Wes and Diane's dock, which is still drenched in sunshine. But still, after only about ten minutes in the water, time to swim across the inlet cove and back, my fingers are icy and white. When I climb out, the heat of the sun is a blessing.

I didn't expect anyone to be here, and no one is. I leave a note stuck in the camp screen door at about eye level. "October 12," the note says. "The bear was here."

In the summer, we drive the mile and a half from our house to where we park the car, then walk the quarter mile through the woods to our camp and small dock at the north end of the pond. But once ice forms, the south end is just twenty minutes away from home by foot, even less when there's enough snow to travel on skis.

I love being at the pond, but I love going to it

too. After a few days and nights of clear, sharp cold in early December, I can cross Temple Stream right behind our house on the inch or two of ice there, swing north through our big hayfield, then into the now nearly snowless woods where the deer can still ramble and feed at will, then across the Mitchells' woodlot and onto the landing where Toby and Weikko Hellgren yarded the wood they cut here, then up over the little hill on the short stretch of truck road that goes from the landing out to the town road. From the little metal grill bridge that crosses the pond outlet, I can see the beaver dam that has raised the water level of the pond about six inches this year. That slightly higher water makes the going from the road into the pond much easier than it usually is before heavy snow comes to level things out. Usually I have to fumble along, feeling my way between hummocks of marsh grass. Now, threaded between the hummocks, is a smooth path of ice I can follow the hundred yards or so to the edge of the outlet bog.

And there, on the pond itself, is ice not perfect for skating but almost perfect for rambling. This ice has been subject to rain and thaws, so it is not that smooth black ice of an uninterrupted deep freeze. It's milky with trapped air bubbles but still clear enough that the cracks in it show up like thin white walls, and I can read how thick the ice is—a good six inches.

I can also read what I take to be spring holes in the pond, too. What else would make these irregular stars or starfish or octupi in the ice? The springs send warmer water to the surface, forming perfect round nuclei from which arms of varying length, number, and writhing complexity radiate, registering how the warmer water spread out when it hit the ceiling of ice forming above it. Or such is my theory. It's lovely what the mind, unfettered by knowledge, can come up with.

There are patches of dry snow here and there, windblown remnants from the occasional light flurries we've had. They make for perfect trot-and-skid ice. I use the patch of snow to trot and get up a little speed; then, when I reach the edge of the snowpatch, I skid out onto the ice. And so—trot, trot, skid—trot, trot, trot, skid—I trot-skid the length of the pond, heading for Wes and Diane's camp.

There, at the north end, the light snow has gathered into a continuous crescent around the end of the pond, and in it are coyote tracks patrolling the water's edge and stopping to investigate the old beaver lodge built right on the edge of the inlet bog.

Later, when ice and woods and hills all lie under a thick blanket of snow, I ski the length of the pond from south to north, then turn around at the mouth of the inlet stream. The landscape lures vision skyward. My eye rambles down the length of the pond and, toward the far end, picks up speed, then races up the ramp of hillsides until, like a ski jumper in reverse, it launches itself from the rounded peak of Derby Mountain and into thin air.

If summer is down-to-earth time, a time when we are preoccupied with everything that grows, swims, runs, and flies down here in the little bowl of hills that holds the pond, then winter is sky time, a time of heavenly preoccupations.

In these darkest days of winter right around the solstice I usually head for the pond about 3:45. The work day is over. Whatever I meant to do today is either done or undone, and now it's time to go see what wonders the fading light will be working at the pond. There's nothing wrong with being out there on the ice at noon, soaking up the sun's heat on a below-zero day, but the experience is static: The sun shines and shines and shines. Or if the sky is overcast, it is gray and gray and gray.

But at sunset, there's no telling what will happen from minute to minute. Tonight, in late December, clouds hanging low in the southwestern sky are picking up patinas of red and gold from the sun already below the horizon. Shadows thicken down here under the pines, but above the string of clouds the sky is clear, and Venus is bright high in the south-southwest. A bit below her and slightly to the north is just the faintest sliver of moon. I can't recall ever having seen one so fine, a slender cantaloupe rind of a moon, a nearly transparent cedar shaving. To call it a "waxing crescent" would be an absurdity, so fine and delicate it is, and fleeting too; for no sooner do I notice it there, just barely skimming the treetops, than it begins to drop below them and is out of sight by the time I reach home.

And twelve days later: a rim of clouds around the

horizon the color of wild trout belly, a deep, fleshy red, nothing flaming about it, a cold-blooded, winter red, and the moon almost directly over-head and bulging out of its first quarter, well on its way toward puffed up full.

Venus is still higher and brighter tonight. At this point in my life, I tend to see lone stars in duplicate or triplicate or with rays of light pro-jecting from them. This, my optometrist tells me, is the result of astigmatism, the eyeballs sagging out of shape after being hauled around in my head for sixty-five years. Well, whatever the rea-son, Venus, my favorite star, my favorite goddess, is always welcome in triplicate. Who can ever get too much of Venus?

Mild, quiet. What bloody noisy creatures we humans are even at our most silent. Here I am, sliding along on wooden skis, and the racket is intolerable. I'm hauling my bubble of noise along with me like a snail his shell or one of those spiders with a big balloon on behind. The only way I can escape the crunch of my poles and skis in the snow, the creak of my leather boots against the metal of the bindings, my own breath, the movement of air in my ears, is to stand stock-still. When I'm moving, I'm my own deafening noise machine.

Tonight, even the most skilled of watercolorists would go mad. He couldn't concoct washes subtle enough to capture all these shades. There's broken cloud cover letting patches of blue sky through, but along the horizon, that rich, deep-sea blue fades into an icier, paler blue. Overhead, tinges of red, pink, and mauve edge into royal purple where the clouds are thickest. Embers glow in the southwest as gray starts settling out of the clouds to the north, and in the fifteen minutes it takes me to go up the pond, turn, and start heading back, gray has covered the northern sky, obliterating the color. By the time I'm off the pond and in the woods, the whole sky is gray. The watercolorist could not have kept up with these rapid shifts, each of them so fleeting that it's impossible to speak of "each of them." What I saw was a continuum. No static art could catch its reality. No motion picture could either because even the widest screen is too small a frame. Art, that poor old stumblebum, just can't catch up with nature.

Over the twenty or more years of my winter visits to the pond at dusk, it has shown me all its moods. The wind may be howling, whipping spindrift up into my eyes, or the air may be clear and still with stars starting to spark way up in the sky as the temperature heads down toward twenty or thirty below zero. But if there is any image that is most like the pond in winter, an image like a characteristic expression on a beloved face, then it is what I see on this evening in late January.

The day warmed slowly after a night near zero. Smoke from the chimney has been heading north all day. The cloud cover has been thickening, as if someone were pulling up one blanket then another on a cold night until, now, the temperature is just a bit below freezing, and the air seems filled with fine goose down.

Standing on my skis in the middle of the pond, I look back onto Derby Mountain, and it is no more than a hazy outline. The air is palpably soft; sky above and snow below shade into each other as the light fades. Which is heaven? Which is earth?

Molly, our neighbor Sandy's dog, is with me tonight and standing now at the edge of the outlet bog. She's troubled by something there yet fascinated by it. My fading eyes cannot penetrate the thickening darkness. I suspect she has scented some creature that gives her pause rather than invites her to the chase. What it is I can only guess. She turns away and bounds across the ice to run ahead of me in my ski trail as I head for home.

How unlike Lucy who always stuck close by me in the last few years of her life. She was my constant companion on these daily winter outings, and I felt bad about them only when the snow conditions were miserable for her. Like one time in her last winter when the snow was slightly crusted and my skis broke the path up into chunks she fell between. She came home lame but was ready to go again the next day. Or when her paws kept filling up with packed snow she would stop to chew out.

I think of her as I ski home, her grave under a red maple down near the garden. Rita has said she would like her ashes buried on Lucy's grave. Why not? And if Rita's and Lucy's are there, where else would I want mine?

Then, some evening in early or mid-February, when I make my turnabout at the inlet bog and head back down the pond, I feel a faint breath of warm air on my face; and the sky in the south is soft and dark, a huge, water-laden sponge ready to start wiping winter away. The sun rides a little higher each day. I can ski out here as late as 5:30 and still have plenty of light to get home.

Temperatures ride up into the forties in the daytime. The lovely, silky powder snow of winter goes to hell in a handbasket, thaws and freezes, turns grainy and icy in the overnight cold, pulpy in the warmth of day. Out on the pond, water wicks up so fast in my ski track that I can't go back on the trail I made coming out.

In March the wind out of the northwest, picking up water from the melting snow, is no longer dry. It smells like laundry hung out on a breezy spring day, sun soaked and wind drubbed. In

April I have to go to the pond in the morning before the sun turns the whole surface to a treacherous mush I sink in over my ankles. To get out onto ice that will hold me, I jump across the narrow moat of meltwater all around the shore of the pond. Soon the water will take over, soaking up through the snowpack like coffee in a sugar cube. The surface of the pond will be black and immobile. We can't get on it with skis; we can't dive into it. If we launch a canoe, we can't go anywhere. The ice is too thin to bear our weight and too thick to let the canoe pass. If we are alert and pay close attention day by day to what sun and wind work here on the pond, we can catch that moment when the sheet of ice disintegrates into candle ice. Then we can paddle everywhere, each stroke setting those clear, hard candles tinkling like a million crystal chandeliers.

But for a few weeks there will be no skiing, no ice fishing, no snowmobiling, no swimming, no boating. Neither we nor anyone else will be able to *do* anything on the pond. Or, rather, all we'll be able to do is contemplate it, which is the most important thing we do here anyway, regardless of whatever else we're doing. Before and after each swim, we stand and look. Even in the middle of each swim, right from water level, we look. In the middle of each snowstorm or each brilliantly clear December evening, we stop and look.

And in May, when the sun has warmed Wes and Diane's porch by late afternoon, we can again settle into the rocking chairs there for beers and conversation. Wherever else our talk may take us, it inevitably circles back to where we are, to what we are seeing. We know that here—on this pond, at this moment, for as long as it lasts—we are living an idyll. Idylls are not a hot literary item these days. They celebrate the peace and simplicity of pastoral existence, things most people can hardly conceive of, much less hope to experience. The very idea of an idyll seems rather quaint and cute, a theme for a costume party maybe, shepherds and shepherdesses cavorting on the green.

But chase a word back far enough and you find there's more to it than meets the eye. In the third century B.C., Theocritus called his short poems about rural life *eidyllia* or "little pictures." *Eidyllion* is a diminutive of *eidos*, meaning "form" or "picture," and that noun goes back in turn to the verb *eidein*, "to see," which is also the root of "idea" and of the Greek *eidenai*, "to know." What the idyll is really about, then, is not a masquerade ball but about seeing and knowing the natural world, living in it and in harmony with it. At Drury Pond the human and the natural coexist in a near perfect balance. The size and topography of the place have set limits on human presence and activity; and, so far anyway—knock wood—the people drawn to the pond have understood those limits as benefits, not drawbacks, of this landscape and been more than content to live within them. So to say we live an idyll at Drury Pond is as literally true as the truth of a word can get, not so little a picture after all but quite a big one, a vision of what could be in the world beyond the pond, if only that world would let it.

SHIP, DREAM, POND, TALK

❧

Wesley McNair

THE SHIP

There could be no better introduction to the camp in Temple, Maine, where Diane and I spend each summer and early fall, than the private road that takes you there. The line of grass at the center tells you the road has nothing to do with the beaten path. Its single lane says this journey is for nobody but you. The corner it takes as it turns off the wider road into the woods stands for seclusion and anticipation.

In free verse poetry the drama comes from an interplay of the sentence and the line, the inquisitive and restless sentence pressing on, and the line, with its image or fragment of thought, tugging back as if to say, "Pay attention to this." The road in, a long, unfolding sentence of trees and green light, has this drama. Around one curve, a patch of high meadow rue and blackberries brush against the car; beyond another, in a dark space, the track widens to avoid a small dip that held water in the spring; up ahead, the road turns yet again, ascending a short hill to disappear. Then there is a clearing where a yellow wagon wheel rests against a birch tree, and the road takes you down to your first sight of the pond.

Rising up through the trees, the pond looks like the sky and, as every visitor sees parking in the driveway and getting out for a closer view, *is* the sky, its reflection printed from the near to the far shore. And there, down among the trunks of birch, spruce, and pine, is the camp. The door of what appears to be the front of the building is actually at the back. The front has been the back of every New England house Diane and I have lived in. What we called the front door of our farmhouse in North Sutton, New Hampshire, was really a side door; the door at the front was seldom used. We enter our current home in Mercer, Maine, through a back door beside the garage; the tall Federal facade and front lawn are on the other side of the house. So it is with the camp. When you have followed the handrails made from straight saplings down the stone steps to arrive there, the front is still farther down, a zig-zag of handrail and stone away.

Is the irony of entrance into the houses of northern New England related in some way to the inaccessibility of Yankees, echoed by the irony and understatement of their speech? I have always thought so. There are practical reasons for making the side or back the front as well, of course, the main one in this case being that the front is where the pond is. Yet entering by the back door, I can never avoid the feeling that the full expression of the camp is being kept even from me as I proceed toward the screen porch and its dramatic view. The mixture of privacy and expectation is delicious.

"It's like a ship," our old friend Malcolm Cochran tells us as we give him a tour on his first visit. Malcolm means how trim and compact the camp is, each area just large enough for its function. The back door opens beside a coat closet with overhead cabinets, then leads to the upstairs hallway, at the left of which are three bedrooms. One of them, a bunk-room with custom-made beds, you pass going down a short entryway to reach the second. Opening the door of the sec-

ond, you find another snug sleeping compart-
ment, with a full-size bed; a half-dresser and
rocker at the bed's foot; a recessed mirror in the
wall above the rocker where books and grooming
accoutrements can be kept; and as deep as the
mirror's recession, enclosed storage cabinets and a
clothes closet. The gas lamp above the bed is perfectly situated for reading; nearby the lamp is a
hook for your glasses when you're ready for sleep,
and a small screw to hang your watch on. Lying
here above the ship's hold, you have the distinct
feeling of being held.

Behind my small typing desk in the hallway,
the next door down, is the master bedroom con-
taining its own strategically placed gas lamp;
a chest and dresser; and to the left just inside the
entrance, the *pièce de résistance*, a fieldstone
fireplace, its stone first appearing below the
woodwork in the outside hall. The upstairs fireplace, with its creamy mortar and variegated rock,

prepares the eye for the larger fireplace which stands directly beneath it in the living room. So there are two simple materials that dominate the interior of our camp: wood and stone. They become textures you touch or rub against moving from one intimate space upstairs to the next. Going downstairs, you reach to a bannister made of peeled fir poles from the nearby forest. Putting kindling and logs in the downstairs fireplace and striking a match, you draw the screen and your hand across quartz and granite gathered just outside. The stones say the same thing the simple and intimate spaces of the camp say: What you require in your life is less complicated than you thought. They say, All you need is right here around you.

On early summer mornings when no fire is necessary except the flame I start for instant coffee on the gas range in the kitchen, I step out onto the porch above the pond for a full view of Drury Pond. Standing there in the prow of the ship, I look out on water always right for the itinerary I have in mind. Tree-lined, with only seven other cottages, mostly unoccupied, the pond calls me away from the world just as the camp itself does. On rainy days a loon pops his head up near our dock, then goes right down under again, as if to demonstrate the pleasures of deep-diving. When the weather is fair, the sun chases clouds of vapor off the pond in perfect harmony with the burner in the kitchen as it brings water for my coffee to a boil. Rain or shine, I take my morning coffee, a notebook, and a pencil to my favorite rocker on the porch, from which I can see three ponds at once: the long curve of water stretching out to Lucy Point and beyond, the encirclement of sky that appears on the pond's surface, and the imagined underworld where the loon goes diving and flying. Opening to a new page, I begin the voyage into me.

DICK'S DREAM

Above the stairs of the camp is a picture of Tor House, the stone structure built by the poet Robinson Jeffers in Carmel, California. I bought the picture—a print of a watercolor—on a California trip Diane and I took to see our oldest son and grandchildren at the same time we were moving into the camp. As I go downstairs watching this lovely print hover for a moment over my head, then pass from view, I often think of the history of Jeffers's Tor house, based on a dream that was fated to disappear.

Just eighty-five years ago when Jeffers arrived at the Carmel coast by stagecoach, it was entirely undeveloped. He later wrote that when he saw the hill of rock overlooking the sea where he would settle and raise his children, it seemed to him "the inevitable place." For the next few years, he built his house and then his tower, lugging many of the stones up from the sea by himself or with the help of his sons. As he constructed the place of rock on rock ("Tor" is the Gaelic word for "stone"), he and his wife added ceramic and stone from spiritual and artistic locations in Europe; created gardens, bordering them with the shells of abalone, a mollusk central to the diet of coastal Indians; inscribed doorways and panels with verse, songs, and classical mottoes that consecrated the mythology of the poetic life. One inscription that was particularly moving to me appeared in the stone near a window in the dining room: the death date of Thomas Hardy.

When Jeffers etched it, in praise and sorrow, the development all around Tor House had long since begun, driving the natural world and its creatures away and making clear to this poet that his dream house was little more than a memorial to the vision which had earlier inspired him. Today, Jeffers's house can be found only after searching the streets surrounding the beach of Carmel. The large picture window on the second floor of a neighboring house looks down into Jeffers's gardens. Imposing structures built by the wealthy are everywhere. One of them, our tour guide told us, has been named "The Inevitable Place."

I can't help but wonder if what happened around Jeffers's house will one day happen around ours on Drury Pond, free as the pond now is of jet skis, motorboats, and on most days, activity on its few docks. For me our camp is a house of poetry, just as Tor House was; for Diane, a jazz singer whose lyrical voice I hear upstairs when she practices in the afternoon, it is a house of song. Inevitable as retreating to this place seems to us, we are only the latest in a series of owners that have valued its unacculturated peace since it was built in the early fifties. The most recent was Dick Vaughan, who sold us the camp after showing me its long shoreline and sharing his stories about loons and a moose he and his wife, Peg, had seen

there. Above the door to the porch he had printed his name for the camp on a square of wood:
"Dick's Dream."

Because Dick, a man in his seventies, had a
heart condition, he asked me to help carry his
canoe to his truck on the day he packed up his
belongings, and when I arrived on the appointed
September afternoon, he told me, a little down-
cast, "I just took my last swim." I wrote him in a
follow-up note, "Come back any time you
please." Sadly enough, he held to his word, dying
six months later. Dick Vaughan's death haunted
me throughout the spring we moved in, for it
suddenly turned the camp and the many things
he had left behind there into his last effects. It was
impossible not to see how much he and Peg had
cared about the place in the stone walkways and
handrails they had installed; their stone-bordered
garden outside the kitchen window, where peren-
nials now sprouted; and the cabinets of the

kitchen itself, painted a bright yellow, with red handles to match the small red hand-pump beside the sink. I thought of the many breakfasts that must have begun with the sound of the coffee-grinder fastened at one end of the cabinets, and of guests served with the cups and dishes inside the doors. Behind other doors there was more of the Vaughan inheritance. In the closet under the stairs, which eventually became our combination oar-storage and pantry, we found a chain lock for a canoe, various hand tools, an organizer of nails and screws in all sizes, and touch-up paint for the kitchen and all the other rooms of the camp. The upstairs closet and overhead storage areas contained sheets, blankets, and sleeping bags; inside the small bathroom off the hall, with its chemical toilet, there was a bureau bearing a colorful array of washcloths and towels.

But the most intriguing treasure was the cache of games and puzzles in well-worn boxes, some dating back to the 1960s. Who could have predicted that entertainments with names like Parcheesi or Backgammon would go so quickly out of fashion with great numbers of Americans? Yet the games we discovered seemed outdated, largely forsaken by a society whose leisure time, quickly vanishing, is spent by watching television, surfing the Internet, or playing video games. What these earlier pastimes lacked was electronics. You started and played them entirely by hand, opening a game board used by two to four people. They were no less interactive than the video game, but their interaction, unlike that of the electronic diversions, was communal. The competition they offered, executed by cards and dice and tokens, involved teasing, goading, defeating, being defeated by, and having fun with family and friends. Their legacy as part of Dick's Dream suggested the loneliness of our pursuits back on the grid, and the need to spend more of our leisure with those we love.

Dick also left behind a folder of plans for a septic system he showed me when Diane and I made our first tour of the camp, thinking they would be an incentive for us to buy the property. All we had to do was provide the camp with electricity, he said, then we could build the system and put in a flush toilet. The lady who owned the upper part of our road wouldn't allow him, he told us, to erect poles for electricity, but since he had managed to get two phones in the camp by running a cable down under the water from a camp across the pond, he didn't see why we couldn't drop an electric cable under the pond. Though we were initially intrigued by the idea, it seemed dangerous and impractical to us in the end, and anyway, Diane and I decided, the camp's pristine outhouse, with its tiled floor and the tufted lid-cover for the hole, was solution enough. After buying the place, we put our potential flush money into the purchase of an adjoining piece of property, increasing our acreage around the pond, and our shore frontage to 720 feet. We did not want more of the grid, which electricity would have brought us, but more of the world off the grid.

Rejecting Dick Vaughan's wish for electricity, I have often thought of his primary motive for installing it: taking the waste away. The small fortune it would have cost him, a retired schoolteacher, to put in his septic system and flush toilet, and pump the daily deposits uphill to a level area off the driveway was apparently worth the satisfaction of being able to whisk the stuff away, out of sight. A friend of mine, Denis Culley, who is a vocal environmentalist with his own outhouse, claims that our problems with the environment begin with our inability to, as he puts it, "live with our own poop." Flushing the poop away so we don't have to deal with it leads, he says, to our irresponsibility toward all the environmental waste we create. We go on from installing our flush toilets to building smokestacks that pipe unwanted gases high into the air above our factories and toxic waste dumps that receive our discarded chemicals—if we can find locations for them far enough outside our own towns. I do not have the answer to our environmental problems, implicated as I myself am in them. Still, keeping the outhouse, where waste remains to decompose, makes me feel a little better about my relationship with the natural world.

In one of the loveliest poems he ever wrote, "The Purse-Seine," Robinson Jeffers speaks of the allure of city lights, likening them to the terrible beauty of sardines being netted at night off the California coast:

> ...the crowded fish
> Know they are caught, and wildly beat from one wall to
> the other of their closing destiny the phosphorescent
> Water to a pool of flame, each beautiful slender body

sheeted with flame, like a live rocket
A comet's tail wake of clear yellow flame....

At our camp we are a long way from urban America. Most summer nights, the only illumination besides the light from our gas lamps comes from a camp across the pond and the moon. Sitting on our porch in the dark, apart from store fronts, blinking towers, and computer screens, I am in an America that is not yet caught. Like Jeffers and like old Dick Vaughan, I concede the attraction of our technological civilization: without that civilization, I would not have the gas that powers the lamps or, for that matter, the computer back in Mercer on which I file my poems once they are completed. Yet like those two other dreamers, I am attracted nevertheless to a world that is more beautiful and more wild.

ON DRURY POND AND IN IT

A pond, my dictionary tells me, is nothing more than "a body of water usu. smaller than a lake." The problem with the definition is that it describes a pond as a static thing, seen on a map or from the air. Looking down on Drury Pond from my porch rocker during our first summer there, I find a body of water whose essence is movement and change. So the responses to it I have written in my notebook at odd hours of the day are very different from one another:

The pond is a place of risings, the sun rising, the trees rising out of their reflections on the water to meet the sun, a fish rising to make ripples in a reflected pine. Birdsong rising.

All afternoon the pond bears the print of the wind changing its mind, swiftly dimpling the water in one direction, then the opposite. Now a long island of crinkle drifts past the camp. On the far shore waves pick up sunlight like shifting constellations, like scores of fireflies.

Before bed I take the dogs out under the moonlight, daytime on an alien planet, everything around me turned to black and gray and loneliness. Beside the canoe small waves wash over the moon as it rests in reflection. Far away on the pond the reflected moon appears again in an eerie strip of light. Inside the camp, I look back through the door's windowpanes and find the strip of light has disappeared; by the canoe the moon, lengthened into an oval, is boiling with waterbugs.

Looking out to the pond this morning, I eventually notice that I am looking through five thin strands of spiderweb flung from the hummingbird feeder to the eaves. Lifting in and out of sunlight, they are less conspicuous than the distant waves, but also beautiful.

What is more peaceable than a canoe resting at the dock in the sunshine as the waves slip gently under it, swaying its cane seats and their elegant crochet of shadow?

A head of clouds moves simultaneously over the distant hill and its exact reflection on the pond. Then almost indistinguishable ripples turn the reflected sky and trees into an Impressionist painting. Across it, a great blue heron flies, startlingly right-side up.

In the gathering calm of twilight I see the image I have learned to look for: blue holes that gradually appear at the end of the point between the trunks of trees which had seemed full and solid before. Through that distance, the mystery of more distance....

But there are times nothing will do but to be a part of the pond's fluctuating life yourself, as happens in this paragraph from my notebook about a canoe trip with my friend Peter Harris:

Paddling out from the dock onto the still pond to travel its length of about a half-mile, we pass the long necks of birches leaning over the water and see the forested hills shift around us, no sound except the water flowing behind from our paddles and canoe. Gradually, the camps to our right announce themselves, Bob and Rita Kimber's first, whose weathered front is barely distinguishable behind tree trunks; then on a steep bank the blond, rectangular front of the Vogel camp, up on stilts; and finally, as we circle the far end of the pond, the small, two-story cottage owned by the Judsons, and near it, an abandoned cabin. The redwing blackbirds are gone from the lily pads of the outlet, but there are Monet-like blossoms of yellow and white floating on the water.

We paddle past them and down to Lucy Point on the pond's other side, not the dramatic jut of land the word might imply but a gentle protrusion, named after Bob and Rita's beloved dog, who often streaked out ahead of them as they all swam toward it from the opposite shore, so anxious was she to reach it. The red camp on the other side of the point and the three others that follow complete the unfolding narrative of pondside dwellings.

Then we are starting down the inlet between more lily pads; then we are poling our way toward the beaver dam like, I tell Peter, the Indian and trapper in a nineteenth-century canvas by George Caleb Bingham. It turns out he is thinking of the very same painting. Back so far in time, our senses tuned to blooming lilies and purple jots of pickerel weed, we re-emerge at the mouth of the inlet not far from the dock where we began, in the pond of the present. As we paddle toward home, the good green roundness of Derby Mountain ascends over the water and descends deep down into it, deep down into us....

Agreeable as canoeing the pond is, nothing can match being in the pond. Our lives as landlubbers require that we travel upright, placing one foot in front of the other and using our arms to help balance ourselves. In the water we lie down, making swishing motions with our feet and using our arms as the fish its fins, or the bird its wings. Moving across the top of the fish's sky, we are as close as we will ever get to the old human dream of flying, as close as we can be to our first life in the womb and our ancient aquatic past in the cycle of evolution. Is it any wonder why swimming offers such deep pleasure, why when we come out of the water, we feel at once rested and transformed?

Our pleasure begins with discarding the clothes required by our life on land, getting down to the skin we were born with. What else can explain the smiles and laughter that always accompany "skinny-dipping" in the dark, or this childlike and joyful expression we have invented for swimming with nothing on? I have seen enough friends and members of my family whoop and holler and splash each other in ponds and lakes to understand that shedding clothes and jumping into the water makes people shed civilized behavior as well and take fresh delight in one another's company. The delight can take unusual forms. Each day we went swimming on his visit last summer, my ten-year-old grandson Kevin surged out to a certain warm spot beyond our dock so he could turn back to me and exclaim, in his comical imitation of an Irish accent, "T'is loovely!"—to which I, arriving second, invariably answered, "T'is grand!"—after which both of us shouted at the top of our lungs, "T'is!"

Then there is the enjoyment of the long swim in the company of a friend or spouse, where one mixes socializing with a variety of strokes, lying on one's stomach to pursue one's course, then rolling over on one's back to enjoy the talk and the view of the retreating shore and the sky. The pond, just narrow enough to travel from one shore to another and back again in a single trip, is made for the long swim.

At four or five o'clock on summer afternoons, dried off from our own swimming, Diane and I often spot Bob and Rita on their way to the opposite shore. If it is four heads we see, they more than likely belong to Bill and Juliet and their dogs, Wally and Desi, all swimming across the pond from the Kimbers' dock, Wally in the lead.

Sometimes after turning back from the other shore, the four heads approach our camp, and the whole gang pull themselves up onto our dock. There the dogs throw themselves into a shake that moves from their hindquarters to their ears and sends our dogs, Charlie and Annie, to the porch door whining and howling. Then all four dogs are romping joyfully off through the trees, and Jules and Bill are settling into chairs on the porch beside us.

On the afternoon I have in mind, it is near the end of our first camp summer, and Juliet is approaching the end of her pregnancy. Sitting in her two-piece bathing suit, she looks as if she is holding a giant egg in her lap.

"She's kicking," Jules says, already knowing that the egg contains a girl. "Can you see it?"

I'm not sure where to look until Bill leans over to point out where the feet are. "She's upside-down," he says, and suddenly I do see it, the tiny signal from inside the egg, understanding now that the reason Jules strokes her wide middle every so often during our conversation is to send her own message, her hello back.

"Isn't it hard to swim when you're carrying all that weight?" I ask her.

"The water buoys me up," she says. "Actually, the only time I'm free of the weight is when I'm swimming."

I imagine Juliet and the baby-to-be swimming at the same time, one outside and the other inside. Then I think about the birth that could happen any day now though it is officially days away, excited, like everyone around me, by this event that will change our two friends from a couple into parents of a new child. Before they go, Diane wants pictures of them, and as they sit together in the two rockers, Juliet in her two-piece and Bill in his trunks, he presses his stomach out a little to help create what is destined to become the most famous snapshot on the roll: Mr. and Mrs. Pregnant.

When they leave, Wally is the first one into the water, and Desi, apprehensive as ever, the last. While Bill and Juliet swim farther away calling him, Desi paces the dock and twitches and wags, becoming so upset that he jumps into the canoe, then out again. But at last he is in the water and swimming into the distance toward the others until they are all, once more, four heads. As they swim farther still, there are six heads: Wally, Bill, Juliet, Desi, and bobbing nearby them, unmistakable in our binoculars, two loons.

Talk

Most of Drury Pond's wildlife is difficult or impossible to see. That there are short-tailed weasels around us we know only because one awful day we found one, a small, exquisite creature our cat had killed and left as a gift outside the camp's back door. We know there are great horned owls because we hear them calling and responding to each other in the darkness with their eerie "who"s. The who*s* that owls hunt—voles, shrews, and rabbits—must therefore be in plentiful supply. If you are outside at night at just the right time, you might see the wake of a beaver as it swims back home with a branch in its mouth under the moonlight. Walking along a pathway in the woods in the daytime, you might find a snake slithering into the leaves, or more rarely, a bright orange newt.

Occasionally Diane and I see moose foraging near Lucy Point, and once we were startled by the presence of a mother and calf, both staring curiously at us from the shore off our own dock. But the wild creatures most evident on the pond during the day are birds. Observe long enough and you're likely to catch, for instance, the gangly and graceful flight of a blue heron as it makes its way across the pond to one end or the other where the marshlands are. Loons are also a common sight. In early summer this year, when two of them were mating, they surprised me with a medley of strange tunes (loony tunes?) consisting of shrieks, sighs, and giggles I never knew loons were capable of. As Diane's petunias sprouted blossoms off the camp porch, hummingbirds appeared in tiny blurs. We have often seen pairs of ducks. And once there was a goose that landed in a tree.

"It's on one of the top branches, just off our shore," Diane told Bob on the phone. "I think it's gone to sleep up there." A member, with Rita, of the regional Audubon Society, Bob had never heard of a goose in a tree. The two of them drove over immediately from their house in Temple to see it for themselves. Sure enough, there on a high branch that seemed too small for it was a large bird with brown wings and an orange bill. Yet by the time the Kimbers arrived to circle the tree and search their bird books, even Diane had begun to question whether it was a goose: its color was too dark, for one thing, and besides, its neck was too straight and skinny. In the final verdict of the Kimbers, the goose was actually a double-crested cormorant. We all agreed as the Kimbers departed that even though Diane had gotten the bird's identity wrong, she deserved full credit for our shared wonder at this being none of us had ever seen on this pond before.

The discovery of wildlife is always more gratifying when you can share it with others, and some of my favorite talk at the camp consists of the agitated whispers inspired by, say, a gaggle of geese—

real ones this time—skidding to a stop at the pond's center, or the sudden appearance of moose. Working on one of the puzzles inherited from the Vaughans with Bob or Bill, I engage in a different sort of talk. In her poem "The Moose," about a long bus journey in Nova Scotia that leads to a more northerly encounter with a moose, Elizabeth Bishop describes the "dreamy divagation" of "an old conversation/ ...recognizable, somewhere/ back in the bus," the voices

> uninterruptedly
>
> talking, in Eternity:
>
> names being mentioned,
>
> things cleared up finally;
>
> what he said, what she said...

The passengers on Bishop's bus talk, she says, "the way they talked/ in the old featherbed/ peacefully, on and on." For me this leisurely and peaceful conversation is also like the kind that happens when people work together on a puzzle, their talk interspersed by comments on the puzzle's progress as someone locates a missing piece of landscape or sky and pats it into place. My guess is that a hundred years ago when the farm women of the region did their quilting or families shelled beans, they conversed this way too. Their hands busy with mechanical activity, they were no doubt free to let their minds roam, just as we are doing our puzzle—as, for that matter, Elizabeth Bishop was when she worked on "The Moose," busying herself with the four-to-seven syllable count of each line while she talked and dreamed her poem's content.

Not all of the conversation at the camp is so peaceful as puzzle talk, but it is frequently wide-ranging and ruminative. I have often thought free verse poets could benefit from listening to the syntax of meditative conversation. When we ruminate aloud, finding with our eyes some area of the ceiling or wall that helps us match the right phrase with our thought, our sentences become longer and more elastic, expanded by words like "and," "but," "if," or "because," and punctuated by stresses of meditation and feeling that resemble the line breaks of free verse. On the porch of the camp in the afternoon, such talk is assisted by cold beer; the view of pond, woods, and sky; and a quiet so pervasive the occasional hummingbird at the feeder may seem too loud. At night in the living room, we exchange our long sentences with guests in the light of the gas lamps that cast shadows on wood and stone. Robert Frost once remarked that poetry is "the art of having some-thing to say," and that the poem's "better half" is "the wildness with which it is spoken." I sometimes hear in our camp talk this wildness— as if we are almost speaking poetry, as if this place wild enough to include a cormorant that sleeps in a tree had entered our speech.

It is no accident, given the natural surroundings of the camp, that our conversations with visitors sometimes turn to the despoiling of nature and the senseless hunting of its creatures elsewhere. It was here Diane and Rita hatched the idea of involving PETA, the organization against animal cruelty, in an offensive to stop the practice of bear-baiting in Maine. On another afternoon Bob and I thought our way beyond the forested hills around the pond to the north of Maine, where every day more of the forest's diversity is cleared away and replaced—when it is replaced—by a narrow range of fast-growing trees that can be quickly harvested. But our talk is typically less somber and a lot less focused. When Diane's close friend Carol Hedden came for dinner, for instance, we covered family relationships; how she got involved with weaving; kinds of falling in love, including falling in love with the house where she and her husband now live; and last but not least, the migration of writers to the Temple area just before she arrived here in the late 1960s.

Since the writers who preceded me in the region included people like Hayden Carruth, George Dennison, Mitch Goodman, Theodore Enslin, and Denise Levertov, most of them poets, I was keen to know all she could tell me about their time here, and circled back to the subject as new questions occurred to me.

"Did they meet with each other regularly?" I asked her, and then, "Was there a central figure in the group?"—wanting to know, and at the same time wanting to see Carol's earnestness as she tried to match my questions with answers, caught in the spell of memory.

"It wasn't like that," she said. "Oh, they knew each other, all right, and they would visit now and then. But there really wasn't any group," she added, shaking her head, "not as far as I remember."

Still, I am inclined to think these writers did more than socialize—that they showed each other work in progress occasionally, just as Bill, Bob, and I do, and that having each other nearby made them feel less isolated by the solitude writing requires. This excerpt from "Questions," a recent poem by Hayden Carruth recalling his talks with the deceased George Dennison, gives proof that their relationship was more than incidental:

Your voice comes to me, George, on the winter night

In the faint mazy stars, a murmur of hesitant light

In the air frozen solid, it seems, from here to Maine.

...What are you saying, George?

I strain to hear. Are you as smart and percipient

As you were, can you tell me what I almost know

In your words not mine as you used to, words

So French and accurate I thought Descartes

And Camus must live in you as well as Tolstoy

And Kropotkin, words of fierce loyalties and loves

for beautiful ideas and men and women?...

In any case, knowing from my own experience how this spot in West Central Maine favors solitude, with its wild places and distance from the world's traffic, I can easily see why the writers came here, and why many of them stayed—most of the rest leaving for other locations off the beaten path. The rest include Carruth himself, who wrote those words to a dead friend at his farmhouse in Munnsville, New York, carrying on his conversation as all writers do, by conversing with himself.

Thinking of the authors who preceded me, and of my writer friends Bill and Bob, I am never quite alone as I conduct my own interior conversation each morning on the camp porch. Besides, I have my dogs Charlie and Annie beside me;

stretched out in the sun, they know that when I hold a tablet in my lap, there is nothing to do but sleep. Most importantly I have the pond, which encourages my writerly talk, just as it once encouraged George Dennison, who wrote in this passage from his book *Temple* of taking his canoe out on the pond and discovering other isolatos like him:

It was early evening. The pond was perfectly smooth and quiet. I paddled the full length of it, watching a beaver swim across.... A very handsome large loon, one we hear uphill at the house every day and every evening, swam placidly not far from me. Redwing blackbirds walked on the lily pads.

Cowbirds

Bill Roorbach

*I*n Maine access to a swimming hole on a nice hidden lake or pond is not limited by any general law but only by no trespassing signs, generally placed on trees along roads one knows are near water by evidence of the quality of the sunlight and sometimes by cheerful stacks of little boards painted with family names and nailed on telephone poles, surmounted by the uncheerful and usually larger sign: private. But even if there are no warnings, it's a hard heart that can walk right down some stranger's driveway to jump in a jewel Maine lake or pond.

The way in for the landlocked, then, is properly through the woods, crunch and snap down through the forest, picking a starting place where there are no driveways, dead-reckon and battle your way downhill (it's always downhill, the last way to water, unless there's a dam involved), hike till the water shines and flashes through the low branches of its trees, and find your own little rock to sit on pondside, or, when the gods are with you, your own little beach at the lake. But that relies on a lot of luck and too much pluck for me most days—usually the spots where there are no driveways only persist in that agreeable condition because down at the water where a driveway would have led there is no proper shore, no place to build a camp.

Most often the hiker ends up wrong side of a beaver bog or in the windward shallows, stiff breeze in the face, wading through muck and leeches thinking whether he can quite dive yet or needs to struggle further. Or you find that you've walked in behind the posting, nicely avoiding the signs (and so enjoying the woods) but not avoiding the trespass, and there's that big fellow raging over in his aluminum rowboat.

Anyway—Drury Pond had been like that for me. Meaning to do a little flyfishing, I'd crunched down through the woods—very steep grade—beaten my way down sometime during Juliet's and my first spring in the neighborhood (our house is three miles downstream; we bought it in 1992), and noted eight camps, one a derelict, the others but one empty off-season, the occupied one proud across the thickest part of the pond high on a bedrock outcrop behind stately pines.

On the shore below that camp and on the boggier shore below its neighbor camp a total of three boats were turned turtle—a canoe and two rowboats. That day there was no breeze at all and the water was the sky and showed its own shoreline diving into the sky.

I wanted a canoe. Here, by God, you'd do well in a canoe. Far off to the left you'd explore a cattail bog, far off to the right an alder bog. Well, *far* is the right word only for the man on foot at the shores of a pond with no fisherman's paths around it (not so rare in Maine, where there are so many ponds and lakes). According to the *Maine Atlas and Gazetteer* map (a tall book of maps, which I'd left back up in the cab of my truck), Drury Pond is something slightly less than half a mile long, two-tenths of a mile across at the widest point. I could swim to any point on its shore faster than I could walk.

As at most unbothered ponds, the trees at this

northwestward shoreline were old and leaned out way over the water, all those decades of seeking light, leaned way out over their own tangled roots, these exposed by winter ice and the multi-centennial splash of small waves. Under water in a pond like this, one sees "dead Indians," trees fallen in and preserved by the cold for centuries, all pointing to the deep center of the pond.

Trees, trees—gorgeous, but really there was no place to get a good cast, and the wading wasn't great. Yuck: a thick, rich, old humus bottom under twelve inches of water that nevertheless put you up to your thighs immediately, so no way to get yourself properly out from under the leaners to fish. Still I tied on a black beetle imitation— just a spot of yellow on it—and pulled in sunfish one after the next, trying not to torture them, popping them off the barbless hook right at the water, not even bringing them quite to hand, enjoying this, and the smell of fish that got on my fingers, and the sharp pricks of their staunch dorsal fins and the wriggle of the little lives inside scales, the furious kicking caudal fin, the heat of life in their rolling eyes. There was also pleasure in the little mind-game of knowing I wouldn't have starved had everything depended on the fishing.

The only places I could see around Drury Pond to cast were the cuts in front of the camps—and I'm just not the sort to stand in someone's yard, whether they are gone or no. Some roll-casting got my beetle out to four or five little yellow perch. A nice afternoon of it. My first Drury Pond day and the last for a couple of years: other places I could get my canoe in more easily; here you'd have to trespass. Drury Pond resisted me, enforced a natural privacy not entirely invented by its lucky landholders.

My next Drury trip was a few Junes hence, after

I'd made the happy acquaintance of Bob Kimber, who is an outdoorsman and a spirited, sunny writer, also a translator and a Princeton Ph.D.— but never mind all that (things he wouldn't tell you right away, in any case), he is Bob and always cheerful and funny, always with a project and a helping hand. He's got a full head of white hair and gray and keeps himself groomed and lives in work clothes a lot and barks with laughter at one's jokes and makes his own great jokes and stands a little wiry and not too tall, gestures when he talks, waves his beat-up hands. He's handsome, too.

This day he has invited me to help him rebuild a friend's simple dock on the pond, their old one having partially sunk and rotted some after many good years of service. Hot day and Bob and I are up to our hips in the chilly waters of June, pulling the old floater free—it's simply built, just spruce boards nailed across two stout trunks of spruce— twelve feet out into the pond, simple as that, and our new design will imitate the old one, do the next twenty years. We pull the old floater free from the chains that hold it (these nailed to roots, ubiquitous Drury Pond roots), then just scoot it along the bank like a submarine coming in for shore leave, just a periscope and catwalk showing, send it along a hundred feet or so where it parks itself under a leaner and will sink over years to join all the dead Indians sunk there, to be preserved like them by the cold.

That particular camp is toward the alder end of the pond, west side, and in June one saw the lily pads floating across the way in bright sun—frog-jump leaves still small, blooms still tight balls. And to the south one saw electric lines, which must follow a road, and the road must cross an outflow stream, that is, pass over a bridge, but the land falls away over there, falls below pond level, which means there is a dike of some sort, a long dam, one would guess, which means beaver work, millennial beaver work, Drury Pond a beaver impoundment, could be 10,000 years old. William Drury and his wife Elizabeth and their six kids didn't get to their Temple homestead till recently, in those terms: 1798. The Drury Pond outlet stream couldn't be very long—it must join the Temple Stream immediately, the Temple Stream which I knew well even then, better now—it flows hidden in its own cut behind the Kimbers' farmhouse not a mile downhill from here in the intervale, then two miles more flows through the pastures below my own, and some of what flows is Drury Pond water.

Bob had already cut trees for the floats and we just splashed them in the pond using a peavey pole (my first time—Bob is always teaching me new things, showing me new tools, generous man), peavey pole and log hook, splash and float and guide, lined the floats up parallel and sawed spruce boards to four feet, nailed these one at a time across the three new floats and pretty soon had a dock to stand on and dive.

After that we took the right of the helpful to take a swim now and again off that dock, I and my wife Juliet, Bob and his wife, Rita, she a Swiss expatriate with wry smile and undependable knees. I mention the knees only because it explains her caution and force with our over-exuberant dogs—one playful tumble into Rita might pop every tendon in sight. And our boys were playful, all right, racing through the underbrush with the Kimbers' Lucy, an elegant little dog, chaser of chickadees (our fellows lean to squirrels), black flags of hair, gone a little white at her snout, distinguished older lady, and a very cheerful swimmer, since flown to her reward. Our Wally is a big mutt, black and white, all chest, a mighty swimmer (the spaniel in him), always has to be in the lead (whimpers piteously if he gets behind), shoulders out of the water. Desmond, our smaller dog—half border collie, half Boston terrier, very handsome despite the odds—Desi is a more desperate swimmer, sinking up to his ears, kicking those little paws, always aimed at the nearest way out but happy to swim nevertheless. The three dogs would gambol and growl and tumble all around Rita's knees till Wally and Lucy hit the water, Wally in the lead, of course, snapping water bugs, and off the two of them would swim while the people among us got down to swimsuits, then one by one leapt or dove or climbed down off of the new spruce boards into water deliciously warm (if the weather had been sunny) or startlingly cold (if it had been raining), and we'd stroke and paddle and kick and glide straight across to the lily pads, turn when the cords of the plant wrapped our feet like seaweed and brought the idea of sinking to mind, brought the ensnarling hair of Undines to mind, those malevolent water sprites of olden Europe who lured sailors, swimmers, drunkards to watery deaths through siren visions of beauty.

What lovely swims we had, the pond suddenly our own. We'd chat a little, our chins in lapping wavelets, then swim hard, an hour or so's outing at the onset of many fine evenings (I believe the Kimbers swam *every* evening; we only joined them occasionally). But then the folks who owned the house turned up, about August, and the dock wasn't ours anymore. Nor Drury Pond, suddenly. Well, there are plenty of places to swim in Maine in August.

One of the camps came up for sale, this availability not the kind of thing normal mortals hear about. But Kimber has his Olympian ear to the pulse of the town of Temple and an eye to the sky and certain mysterious soulful links to Drury Pond, and had long wanted his own bit of shoreline. So pretty soon I was lucky enough to be helping Bob finish building his own little dock down the hard slope from his camp, an older, hand-built cabin with chimney about to fall (it has done so since) and outhouse tilted, lovely porch reaching out into the trees on stilts incompletely stoned-in for a basement beneath, a rustic place, complete with a couple of hundred yards of shoreline that includes one of the Drury Pond beaver lodges (at the mouth of a brook), west side of the pond, not far from where I stood fishing those years before. Access is a long and finally steep twitch road, little used, two grassy lanes not for just any all-wheel-drive vehicle, in fact in Bob's vision for foot traffic only, and once in awhile for his old Ford tractor.

Bob has invited me down to help with the dock with his usual generosity. He won't need my help all that much, but knows the little help I'll give will earn me a lowered-guilt family ticket to come swimming summer evenings just this lovely trio of miles from home.

When I get to the camp, hammer in hand, the dock is about built already, spruce boards, once again, but on a standing frame, and with a ladder. Wally has preceded me and is already halfway across the pond, zigzagging after water skeeters and dragonflies, no competition for first place to distract him into straight lines. Desi greets Bob effusively. And Greg Kimber is there, too—didn't see him at first—home from his on-his-own adventures and up to his chest in the pond, holding boards for his dad. Of course, there's the usual father-and-son-doing-a-project-together tension in the air. I bark out jokes to make room for my presence. "Let me stand on your shoulders, there, Greg," stuff like that, not really funny at all, but funny enough.

And Greg wades up out of the water. He's built slender like Bob, his hair long, his head full of gardening knowledge and good dreams of communal living and community life. He's a serious young man but good-humored. One feels well observed by him, but never judged. The dock's about finished when we hear the first rumbles of thunder. The pond goes all dark, flat and smooth, then suddenly erupts in wind devils and then white-caps. Boom and crack, the storm is upon us, first drops falling, pond leaping up to meet the sky.

"Let's get in the water," Greg says wryly.

We hustle up to the shack, a few seconds scrabbling up the hill, but we're soaked down by the time we're inside. Desi trembles, presses up against my leg, quavers and whimpers, pants grotesquely. Wally, oblivious, just likes being with everyone, wags his tail, looks for a hand to scratch his ears. The rain redoubles. The surface of the pond goes invisible—it's all rainfall. Only the big white pines exist out there anymore, and the rain, the rain, the rain crashing down, close lightning, boom again, and crack. Desi quakes. But it's energizing, the storm, pure gaiety. The porch roof, which is also the porch ceiling, begins to drip a little, then to actually leak, then to rain upon us.

"Roof is pretty good," Greg says.

Bob's thinking, already coming down the hill on his tractor with a load of shingles and rolls of tarpaper and two ladders and ropes and maybe someone to help.

After that good day, Juliet and I and the boys swim off Bob's dock and never have that feeling of being somewhere we shouldn't, somewhere someone else considers private. We swim across Drury Pond nearly every day in summer, sometimes with the Kimbers, often not, dogs in the lead, Juliet next, I always following, swim across to sit on a big rock over there in the sun, get warm, return, the widest part of the pond, not quite a quarter mile, no lily pads, often a loon diving nearby then surfacing nearer, diving, surfacing farther, diving, surfacing unseen. Wally pursues for a time, but soon returns to dragon flies and water skeeters—he'll never, ever get near a loon.

And after the swim if the mosquitoes aren't too bad we just stand on Bob's dock and watch the water and maybe talk a little about the work of the day, what I've planted, what Juliet's painted, what Bob is writing, how Rita's knees are holding up, how the various gardens are doing, what books we're reading. It's a very sturdy peace and with the exercise a bright one, bringing mind and body together into one pure thing. Some evenings a beaver swims by a hundred feet out, close enough to inspect us, get a sense of us. It swims past slowly, as if nonchalant, but subtly tilts up its head, sniffs the air, knows us for who we are.

One evening when we are just Juliet and me and the dogs, I chance to look up. High, high above us there are dark birds working insects. At first I think swallows—but these are not swallows.

Too big, though it's hard to judge size against nothing but clouds. The white spots on the underwings are unique—I take note, then look in my bird book at home: night hawks, bearded birds, not properly hawks but whippoorwill relatives, night hawks wheeling, diving, my first sighting ever. Drury Pond gives one these gifts.

The walk back up the trail from the Kimbers' is always sweet and quiet. One looks for mushrooms in the edges of the trail, looks for warblers in the firs, for lady's slippers in the leaf mold, for newts in the wet spots, for squirrels to chase, finds them all, this paradise.

So Drury Pond had accepted me, but only as a guest. And even as the guest of someone so generous as the Kimbers, I felt like Odysseus on Circe's island, or less exaltedly, Nick Carroway at Gatsby's, or less yet, the neighbor kid at the house with a pool, or worse, a servant invited to Cinderella's ball (not even the char girl herself!), or lower even, the bride's brother's buddy who happens to be in town, or lower yet, a temp worker at his desk among dot-com millionaires. Lowest of the low: a cowbird egg in a warbler's nest.

And you know, you don't want to bug your host, don't want to take advantage, don't want to be there every second, never give them a minute to themselves. The Kimbers, bless them, they had their own routine of swimming every late afternoon. So Juliet and the dogs and I swam elsewhere often—the Sandy River especially, sometimes further away: Long Pond, Porter Pond, Clearwater Lake. But Drury had charms like no other: its calm, its containment, its leaning trees. And was close to home, as well. Juliet and I tried coming later than Bob and Rita might, but that gave us the feeling of *avoiding* them, which was not our plan at all, though it was awkward nevertheless to run into them unannounced. Awkward for us, anyway: Bob and Rita didn't seem to mind. Except maybe at times the rambunctious dogs, who can't check their ecstasy at seeing the Kimbers, and who launch into sarabandes of delight, a barkanalia. Wally particularly is in love with Bob, having stayed with them during a long trip Juliet and I once took, moons over him, wants to eat him up, climb in his pocket.

And it's always Wally in trouble. One of his worst transgressions was of a late summer's evening, air warm, sky already coming dark, when Bob spotted a large snapping turtle swimming under the dock. I saw it, too, and we pointed and exclaimed and Rita came to look but never did see the turtle because our interest in the water right there caught Wally's interest and he leaped in just where the turtle was. Oh, *Wally!* Rita said, genuinely pissed. She had wanted to see that turtle!

I felt like a cowbird chick. I was a cowbird, all right.

It's not that I dreamt of owning a Drury Pond camp—that was too much to ask—but I hatched this plan: access. I especially wanted to get down to the pond with my canoe and do a little fishing without imposing on the Kimbers in any way. I'd heard from several neighbors—erroneously, as it turns out—that the pond was stocked with brookies, and Bob had mentioned pickerel, too. And a morning of perch ain't bad either.

So what about the outlet brook that flowed down to the Temple Stream over the lip of the ancient beaver dam? What of that? On the way home from our next Drury Pond swim, I had a look, drove up the dirt road that passes by the end of the pond, that passes along the top of what amounts to a dike, a dike built by *rodents*.

I drove slowly. You couldn't see Drury at all through the thick alder leaves, but the alders were growing just there precisely because water was near, growing there soaking their roots in boggy percolations. The outlet stream, though, flowed nicely, flowed mildly but visibly under a little steel-deck bridge which was not much more than a long section laid across the stream's banks. I stopped on the bridge, looked down happily. The water was four feet below, but looked pretty inviting, wide as the canoe was long, deep enough to paddle, mildest current.

Juliet was game. We'd take the next beautiful morning off from projects. And that morning came a couple days later, a Thursday in July. We made a lunch—nice sandwiches and carrots and chocolate cookies, jugs of water—packed that and two big old towels and our swimsuits and a picnic blanket in the wetbag, also lots of other stuff: fly rod, fishing vest, length of rope, notebook, paddles, life vests, bird book, binoculars (two pair), drawing pad, plenty pens and pencils.

We had ourselves a perfect day, clouds at the horizon only, puffs of dreams unmoving. To Drury Pond! On our own terms! Drury ho!

And off we went, leaving the dogs home, poor beasts. But they'd be havoc in the narrow stream, and havoc with lunch. I parked the old truckeroo in a spot that had been parked many times, a little turnout. And breathlessly (I'm always breathless at a new canoeing place—scared of naiads), *breathlessly* I pulled the canoe off the truck, flipped it onto my shoulders, tipped it up to see out a little. What I saw was Juliet, looking like a model in her thrift-store bellbottoms and spangly top, her sassy new haircut sharp at her shoulders, all that blond thick hair flashing in the sun, game smile flashing, too, got the paddles and life vests while I carried the canoe on my head. "Nice hat," she said, old joke.

"Nice haircut," said I, no master of the come-back. I mean, her haircut was nice indeed, why would I make fun?

At the bridge I just plunked the canoe (a Mad River Explorer, chunky, funky, well used), plunked it down off my shoulders with a bounce, slid it bow first into the Drury Pond outlet stream, one smooth motion till I had to let go and the little boat tipped sideways, splashed in on its edge, taking a large gulp of water over the gun-wale. So haul it up by the bow line, tip it, drip it, drop it correctly, guy it up to the bridge length-wise. And it just fit bank to bank, measuring the bridge and the outlet stream precisely: sixteen feet.

Juliet dropped the paddles into the boat, dropped the wetbag and the layers of other stuff, then considered how to climb in. This would be no mean trick, with the canoe floating wobbly under the bridge. She lay down on the steel deck-ing, swung her long legs out over the void, waved her feet experimentally over the canoe, kicking but reaching nothing. She swam her arms then and we laughed until it wasn't so funny, she kind of stuck there on the bridge with her legs waving, her chest and belly pushed into the steel decking uncomfortably. Finally she made her move, lowered herself a notch, kicked the gunwale, pushing the boat farther under the bridge and out from under her. I pulled the painter in the very nick of time as she dropped, she not realizing the boat was in motion under her, a perfectly timed, supremely lucky motion that brought the gunwale back under her foot, past her foot exactly as she dropped.

"Perfect," I said.

"Cake," Juliet said.

She brushed at her bellbottoms and at her spangly top as I turned the canoe upstream using that bow line, turned it upstream with some force to get it moving, hopped in myself as the boat headed pondwards, leapt in what would have been a perfect graceful motion if I hadn't missed the wicker seat trying to sit, missed so as to fall on my butt on the bottom of the canoe behind the seat, my legs arched *over* the seat, my head back on the stern board.

"Earthquake?" Juliet said.

"Just another new way to do things," I said.

"I'm hungry," Juliet said.

"We've got a nice lunch," I said. "Thanks to you."

"Stop here and eat? We could sit on the bridge."

She is funny. And we sort of laughed, but sort of it wasn't that funny, since it was noon already and I was hungry too, starting to get that impatient feeling you get around the undertrained wait staff at resort restaurants. But we were off in the perfect day, perfect hungry happiness knowing that the pond was not a hundred yards away, lunch imminent, then maybe a swim. We paddled. The alders all around the outlet stream were thick, much chewed and trimmed by beavers, dense and forbidding. You'd never get a canoe through that in a million years even though flat water stood around them, never get through there at all without the stream and its beavers having cut this right of way, having cut their own little permanent channel in what I gathered was a kind of sub-pond a degree of altitude lower than the main pond's surface. There must be a beaver dam ahead. And there must be another dam behind, the one forming this dead water, the actual main dam forming Drury Pond, which must be somewhere out of sight below the steel-deck bridge just before a mild fall to the Temple Stream.

The channel made a small turn in the dense alders, and sure enough, we were coming up on a beaver buffer dam, freshly topped. Bob had recently remarked on the pond's level being higher than normal, and here (along with recent rains) was why: the beavers had added about six inches of material to their secondary Drury dam—it crossed the channel here and continued on, sinuously, as far as I could follow it through the alder thicket, the whole construction backing water very calmly, just quietly holding back the whole top six inches of Drury Pond (how many gallons would that be? How many pounds?). I bumped the bow of the canoe and thus Juliet up to the damworks, but she just sat, staring ahead, nice strong shoulders from years of swimming, thinking about something so very important that she didn't notice we'd paused, didn't even notice the bump.

So I stared too, not to disturb her, admiring the dam some more, the flat surface of pond slightly higher than the water we floated on at present, this long present moment, these beaver sticks chewed and stripped and pale (and at that moment looking strangely delicious), these alders around us, this blue sky above, great white arks of cloud forming, Drury Pond ahead. After several hundred heartbeats, Juliet noticed we were stopped.

"Get on out?" I said.

"Not on your life," she said.

"Just climb up on that bigger log there."

She didn't so much as twitch a muscle toward the bigger log. "'Just climb up on that bigger log there,'" she said, quoting me precisely.

So I turned the whole boat, backed myself up to it, and precariously climbed out, one foot then the other on that bigger log. I didn't want to damage any of the beaver works, but wouldn't—the toothy ones had placed this thick log of popple atop the masterworks here, and this bit of inspired engineering I found I could stand on, full weight, without influencing it in any way. From that perch I bent to grasp the gunwales of the trusty canoe, turned it till Juliet was right there beside me, took her hand, pulled her up and onto the log with me. There the two of us teetered, quickly hustling the canoe over the dam (much shallower on the upstream side), over the dam and into the higher water, like going through a lock from one world to the next.

Back into the boat, and onward.

But the channel is far less defined than it's been in its first hundred yards. In fact, now there are two distinct channels, one straight ahead (which peters), one hard left, to the west. We paddle on against the mild current, bearing ourselves ceaselessly into the sky.

The clouds, lovely, seem to be getting bigger, taller, grander, grayer. And suddenly a full-figured one blocks the sun. I'm chilled just as suddenly, feel my feet damp in the well of the canoe, and the chill walks up my legs.

But westward ho! Lunch awaits!

We paddle through the continuing maze of alders, north a ways, seeing glimpses of the pond, then a little east, then north again, then hard west. The false channels are so short we don't have to follow any. But the real channel has gotten shallow, and we're often scraping aquatic grasses, the water slower over them, pushing instead of paddling. Finally we're out of the alders and into the light of the pond—the pond!—oh, it's lovely, not twenty yards away if one could walk or fly. But the channel ends. Sedge hummocks stand in our way like humped dwarfs. The water all around us is filled with grasses and thick with dead leaves.

Decision made, I say, "I'll pull us right to the pond and just dry off later."

And hook a leg over the gunwale, gingerly disembark, one foot on a hummock. The hummock flops sideways while my other foot forces the canoe away. I go into a split that can only be corrected by hopping awkwardly off the hummock and into the water, which is cold, too, and knee deep, then thigh deep suddenly, lapping my cutoff shorts. Juliet turns to see what all the commotion has been. "'Pull us right to the pond!'" she says, quoting me again.

I laugh and hold the gunwale and take a step, which brings me up on something submerged, back to knee deep. The pond is just there—just those twenty yards. I push the canoe over the grasses in water and get about ten feet further, stepping carefully, perhaps walking the length of a huge old log, perhaps walking the spine of a sea monster—the leaves and muck are too thick for me to see my feet, though the leaves and muck are plain to see through the clear top layers of water. A tornado of silt emerges at each slow step. The sun comes out. "Let's eat on those rocks over there," says Juliet, pointing—a short paddle across the pond, nice rock next to the closest camp, the camp with the homemade roll-out dock in full hot sun—so inviting, so close. I step again, step right off my sea-monster log, sink thigh deep. Another difficult step, pushing the canoe and Juliet ahead of me, and it's just a little deeper, though the bottom looks the same—loose leaves, tornadoes of silt, a foot deep. But I'm sinking. Slowly, slowly, I'm in up to my belt. "I'm sinking here," I say.

Juliet looks back, says, "Hurry, then." She's kidding. I think I detect some concern in the changing lineaments of her face.

But I sink some more, up to the bottom edge of the photo of Big Bend National Park on my t-shirt. Juliet's wryish face gives way to an alarmed face. "Stop sinking," she commands. She doesn't want to have lunch alone.

I've got hold of the gunwale of the canoe, so I don't think I'll go under if it comes to it, but I can't pull myself out of the muck because my weight tips the boat too much. I'm up to my nipples. Calmly, or at least trying to speak calmly, I say, "Do you think you can pull the canoe up a little? Maybe paddle some or push with the paddle or something along those lines and get the stern over me?" If I can hook my arms over the point of the stern, I can pull up against the whole length of the canoe, and Juliet's weight. Her spangly shirt glints in the sun. She sticks her paddle in to test the depth, and it sinks in muck, too. And then she paddles, giving it a good go. In fact, she thrashes the pond surface, but the boat is hung up just enough on grasses that only pushing off the bottom is going to work. But there's no bottom. Now I'm up to my shoulders, and that's really enough. I grab the gunwale, say, "lean hard to starboard."

"What does starboard mean?" Juliet says calmly.

"Toward the pond," I say. "At least in this case."

"Your hair is going to be ruined," Juliet says.

And if you've seen my hair you know that this is very funny. We start giggling as my scraggly ponytail goes in, too, and then my chin. I think of Ken Kesey's *Sometimes a Great Notion*, that unforgettable climactic scene in which the burly logger is trapped under water by a whole tree trunk in a flood, caught under there but in contact with the living world, holding hands with his brother, who's helping him breathe through a reed, and our man is breathing through this reed and has every chance of survival (the floodwaters are receding), but he just can't stand it and he *laughs*, laughs and laughs and laughs till he runs out of air and drowns, right at his brother's feet, his poor brother unable to help him, laughing too.

But Juliet and I laugh because I'm up to my lips now and still sinking and Juliet's leaning and I'm pulling hard on the gunwale, tipping the boat hard my way despite Juliet, tipping the boat with my greater weight and really the weight of the bottom of the pond, which is the weight of the entire planet, and the boat's tipping and Juliet is leaning and I can feel my fake Teva's straining at their cheap straps and I can feel my shorts coming off, but pull myself mightily, glad my arms are strong, pull down on the canoe, Juliet leaning further yet, I pulling hard, drawing my knees up in the horrible muck, pull, grunt, pull, increments of nothingness as the planet lets me go, pulling, breathing, trying not to laugh anymore though Juliet is wracked with giggles, pull myself stinking chthonically, popping suddenly right up and into the boat on top of the wetbag, which sudden action prompts a sudden reaction: Juliet almost flops in, too. But she grabs the opposite gunwale and saves herself. Whoosh! I'm alive and only wet to the neck. I scrabble around and get back on my seat. "Your turn," I say.

I'm freezing.

"Lunch?" Juliet says.

We sit a long time, just looking at Drury Pond. It's right there, lapping the last ridge of hummocks and sticks and bog matter only fifteen yards from the bow of our boat, and surely there's a way to do it, but. But. But we're starving. There's an ancient, ancient stump off to port twenty feet. "We've got a hundred feet of line in the wetbag," I say. I point to the stump, thinking how somehow you might lasso it and use it to pull boat and all to a firmer bottom.

"No," Juliet says. She doesn't even want to hear any of my stupid plans.

I retrieve my paddle from the well of the canoe, push on a hummock to starboard, free us from the grass trap, and we back away from our one chance to make Drury our own. We paddle backwards a hundred feet or so till there's a false channel we can turn in, and we do turn, and head back the way we came, looking one more time at each small channel to be sure, but there is no path to the pond. So back over the beaver dam, locking down to the sub-pond level, then to the bridge, and climb out of the boat, onto the steel deck, nicely solid. Pulling the boat back up by the bow line I feel that my arms are sore. Both arms, some funny muscle used only for bog self-rescue, placed there by God for bog pulls only, just in case, and on this fateful day I had to use 'em, ow.

We get everything loaded and it's two o'clock before the cowbird chicks are unpacking a soggy lunch on the Kimbers' dock in shivering shade under growing clouds. And the sandwiches are very good, the carrots terrific. The chocolate cookies are the best ever made or conceived.

Last bite and the sun comes back long enough to dry the mud on my legs, long enough to warm me so I can strip and dive in.

Drury Pond!

My friend Wes McNair, poet and professor, a lovely man the height and shoe size of a basketball star, eyeglasses of a poet, eyes of a poet (basketball skills of a poet, too), all gentle intelligence, long hands, New England to the bone yet tender (he's full of hugs, our Wes, no frost there), tells me with some excitement that a camp is for sale on Drury Pond. From what he tells me, it's the one on the property adjacent to the Kimbers', the only camp on the north end of the pond, the only one with southern exposure, the flag camp, we've called it, because the people there fly an American flag. Wally and Desi have made quick reconnaissance missions down there adjunct to our walks to the Kimbers'. But we cowbirds—Juliet and I—we've only looked off the bluff where the leafy two-track driveways part in a Y.

Now Wes's wife, Diane, singer and librarian (though not at the same time, one hopes), vegetarian cook and gardener (these related), Yankee wisdom, Yankee clarity, Yankee skepticism (that's our Diane), but full of a kind of un-Yankee, fully generous, marvelously melodious laughter, Diane gets behind the project, and before you know it, it's done. There's been no realtor, there have been no ads, there's been the word of only one mouth: Bob's. A national bank won't cough up the money, but our lovely local savings bank doesn't hesitate, and the McNairs' camp mortgage is secured.

That first summer Juliet and I are in heaven— Drury is a pond of friends, suddenly. We visit the Kimbers' still to swim, sometimes in their company, as often not. Our welcome at the McNairs' new camp seems equally large, but still, we don't want to wear it out, or wear the McNairs out, especially in these first months of their ownership.

Juliet's got news, too: she's pregnant with our first child. In July it's seven months, August eight, and we lumber down the hill to the camps. In the water Juliet is still a porpoise—swimming is her favorite pregnant exercise—she's buoyant and round, full of this girl who will be born in September. Back stroke and the belly is prominent, looms out of the water, shines in the sun, you can't believe how large. But still Juliet swims faster than I can, and stays in longer. No danger of her sinking. She wears her same old two-piece throughout the pregnancy, slings the bottom piece low under her enormous belly, something she's learned watching me dress all these beer-belly years (I'm shaped like a basketball *fan,* but the swimming should help).

The swimming, the swimming. The swimming is the same as ever in some ways—except that now you look over at the flag camp and see the people there and feel somewhat under their gaze then realize that the people there are—Wes and Di! It's only a matter of five or six swims before we decide to swim over to their dock to say hi, pull ourselves up to barking dogs (Annie, Charlie), let leap our own barking dogs from the water. Wes comes down bearing camera and gets great shots—of Juliet and me side by side with Elysia inside Juliet, our two glistening bellies in sunshine, the sunshine of their dock, our first Drury sunbathing, in sight of the Kimbers' shady dock. And Di comes down in bathing suit and Wes strips down to his from his great height and you realize these dear friends have legs you've never seen in the decade you've known them and entire bodies. And even on the threshold of sixty human years these bodies are beautiful, and Diane gets a noodle and wraps it around her ample self and floats off, learning to swim, buoyant as hell ("Boobs *float*," she calls merrily). And Wes swims out into the pond saying how cold but stays in long, gets his exercise.

Then we cowbirds swim away, I first, slower and impatient, Juliet next, fast and full, Wally a gargantuan leap from the dock and passes me instantly and snaps bugs and gone off on his many missions: loons, water skeeters, drifting scents. Desi, though, Desi would just as soon not *leap* in but can't figure the best way to get closer to the water so he can be dainty about the thing. He barks and cries piteously, leaps from dock to canoe to dock and back again, not heeding Wes's advice ("Over here, over here, Desmond!") not heeding Diane's ("Desi, you big dumb mammal, down here!"), but pacing and whining and finally not jumping at all but having a brainstorm, spin and run back off the dock, spin and run, *race* us barking back through the forest, no slow swimming for him, no contest. He has to wait a long while but meets us gaily at the Kimbers' dock when we arrive. There we dress.

We come to the McNairs' by land, too, come and do jigsaw puzzles; we eat, we drink, we talk— it's a place to talk (Wes has said). We see the

McNairs' visitors, get their talk, too. Sometimes the visitors are the Kimbers, and then it's a Drury quorum. So good to have all these friends so close and on water.

And we swim—from Kimbers' to McNairs'. At McNairs', we pull up on the dock and Wes and Di come down and we drip and chat and grow chilly; we dive in then and swim away, four heads. We're pond people, very nearly. We come with my dad when he visits and we come with Juliet's folks when they do and one fall day we even sneak onto the porch when no one is home so Juliet can sit in a rocking chair to breastfeed Elysia Pearl, newly arrived. We come for dinner, and we come to see the new stove (Kimber has helped install it), and we come to see the weasel the McNairs' cat, Roo, has killed; we come just to be there. The evenings are best, as fall comes in and swimming is over for the year. One looks out across the pond and sees only sky (as Wes has pointed out), one sighs with the thought of winter.

One afternoon I pop over and it's just Wes and me and we talk and eat peanuts and drink small sips of whiskey and then beers. In the failing light Wes points out a particular camp down the way, the modest camp across from where Bob and I once built a dock together, the plain-hewn camp with rocks I often notice, with trees where the heron roosts, the camp with the homemade dock on rollers: "I haven't seen many people there this summer—not once this summer have I seen those people. It's an older gent. And his daughters are grown and gone off and have better things to do. You know that kind of thing. Could be, just maybe, who knows, they'll be wanting to sell soon."

I think of Elysia jumping from the old hand-made dock into the sky down there. Think of all our heads bobbing through the water over to

Kimbers', thence to McNairs', thence home again. Fire in the hearth, pot of soup in the fire, feet on the stool, book in the lap. Juliet making watercolors. No phone, no power, outhouse mildly fragrant. Elysia playing jacks with a friend out on the moss, five or nine or twelve years old, sixteen. Kissing her boyfriend out on the moss. Just a vision, that's all. Not a premonition. Certainly doesn't mean I'm going to be able to buy any camp, not even that nice old one over there on Lucy Point. Not even that nice one over there under tallest white pines with dock not even rolled out this summer, not even once.